THE
Secret
Switch

Written by **Julie Fitzgerald & Jayla Perez**
Illustrated by **Elena Stowell**

First edition 2025

Published in Canton, GA, USA
by thewordverve (www.thewordverve.com)

Paperback ISBN: 978-1-956856-86-6

Library of Congress Control Number: Forthcoming

Illustrations by Elena Stowell
www.elenastowell.com

Interior and Cover Design by Robin Krauss
www.bookformatters.com

Dedication

For everyone living with Parkinson's and the families who walk beside them . . . your courage inspired us to write this book. May your voices be heard and your journeys honored.

To the researchers tirelessly seeking a cure . . . may your discoveries bring hope ever closer.

To my dear friend and mentor, John Humphreys . . . thank you for teaching me how to stand up, speak out and advocate for Parkinson's awareness with strength and compassion. You were more than a mentor—you were my very best friend. Your steady encouragement, unwavering support, and belief in me, helped me find my voice.

You will always be missed. I hope this book helps carry your spirit forward.

— Julie

Hey there, friends!

We made this book just for you (yep, grownups too!) to help explain something called Parkinson's. It's kind of like a surprise box—sometimes wobbly, sometimes wiggly and full of hmmm . . . what's happening now? But guess what? It's also packed with love, laughter, and little adventures.

This story comes from real questions that I, Jayla, asked my super awesome grandma, Lola Julie. She's the best at turning big stuff into easy-peasy stories that make you feel safe and smiley inside.

And if you have your own big (or little!) questions, don't worry-we've saved some special pages at the end of this book for you to write them down and ask your person with Parkinson's.

So, grab a cozy spot, snuggle in, and let's explore how life with Parkinson's might be a bit bumpy, but also full of giggles, hugs, and heart-squishy moments.

Meet Me and My Lola Julie!

I'm Jayla, and this is my grandma, Lola Julie. Did you know "Lola" means grandma in the Philippines? Cool, right? We do everything together—Legos, jigsaw puzzles, and sneaky snack runs (shhh, don't tell my dad).

But there's something special about Lola Julie: her hands shake, and sometimes she moves slower than a turtle on a skateboard. That's because she has something called Parkinson's disease.

What Is Parkinson's Disease, Anyway?

Parkinson's is a condition that makes the brain send out funny signals. It's like when your TV remote doesn't quite work right, but instead of changing channels, it makes people shake, wobble, or move slower. Some days are harder than others, but everyone with Parkinson's is different kind of like snowflakes.

My Big Questions

When I first saw Lola Julie's hands shaking, I was a little scared. But then I thought, "If I have questions, other kids might too!"

So, I asked Lola Julie everything that was on my mind (and I mean *everything*).

Things like:

> *"Lola Julie, does it bother you when people sometimes stare at you?"*
> *"Why do you walk so slow?"*
> *"Why does it take you so long to tie my shoes?"*
> *"Why are you too tired to play with me sometimes?"*
> *"Does Parkinson's hurt?"*

And guess what? Lola Julie loved answering my questions.

She taught me that it's always okay to ask if you're curious or worried—but just remember to ask privately, politely, and respectfully.

Lola Julie's Superpower— Her Battery

One day, while munching on pancakes, Lola Julie said she needed a "battery change."

Wait . . . what? A grandma with a battery?

Turns out, she wasn't joking. She showed me the tiny bump under her skin where her superpower lives.

The battery powers something called Deep Brain Stimulation (DBS). It's like a brain coach that helps her tremors and to move better. Her battery isn't like the batteries in toys. It's flat and made especially for her DBS. She let me feel the wires under her skin connecting the battery to the Deep Brain Stimulator.

It's cooler than it sounds, I promise. It's her Secret Switch!

8

Wobbles and Giggles

Lola Julie sometimes bumps into stuff or gets shaky. Once, while we were playing, we both tripped over each other's feet and landed in a giggling heap. Daddy wasn't impressed, but we were fine-just a bit bruised and very amused.

Life with Parkinson's can be silly if you let it! Now we are more careful so we don't end up in a giggling heap. And that makes my Daddy happy.

Tremors, Like Tiny Earthquakes

Have you ever felt an earthquake? That's kind of what tremors are like, but in Lola Julie's hands, legs, and feet. Sometimes she loses her balance but doesn't fall over. We call it being "wibbly and wobbly." It makes us laugh-even Lola Julie!

I hold my grandma's hand sometimes when we take walks. It makes me feel like I'm helping, and I think she likes it!

I even use a lid on my cup so she doesn't feel like she's the only one who needs a lid. I don't want her to be embarrassed.

We even have silly straws because . . .
well, we are silly!

12

Helping Lola Julie Stay Strong

Lola Julie says the best thing for Parkinson's is exercise, stretching, and laughing. So we go for walks, do yoga (well, we try) and play games.

We also play racing video games. Lola Julie isn't very good, but she has fun racing me, and we laugh a lot when she ends up in the water and can't get her kart to go where she wants it to go.

Lola Julie says she will beat me one day. She is so determined; she might just do it!

These activities help keep my grandma's mind and body active. On days when she feels tired, it's fun to cuddle up on the couch, eat popcorn, and watch a movie.

Lola Julie the Adventurer!

Did you know Lola Julie hiked across Sicily, Italy, for nine days to raise awareness for Parkinson's?

She climbed mountains and crossed rivers. She hiked 120 miles and nearly melted in the 115-degree heat.

She's like a superhero with hiking boots!

15

NEVER GIVE UP-EVER!

Laugh often - laughter really IS the best MEDICINE!

Be kind - you never know who might need it.

Always hold hands (even if they're wobbly).

Life Lessons from Lola Julie

Lola Julie taught me that everyone has challenges. Some you can see, and some you can't. She says the best thing we can do is be kind and patient with each other.

Oh . . . and **never, ever give up.**

Big and Little Questions

You might be wondering why someone moves a little differently, needs more rest, or does things in a special way. That's okay! Questions help us understand and care better.

What are you curious about? Write your questions here:

1.

2.

3.

4.

5.

Want to draw your questions instead? Go for it!

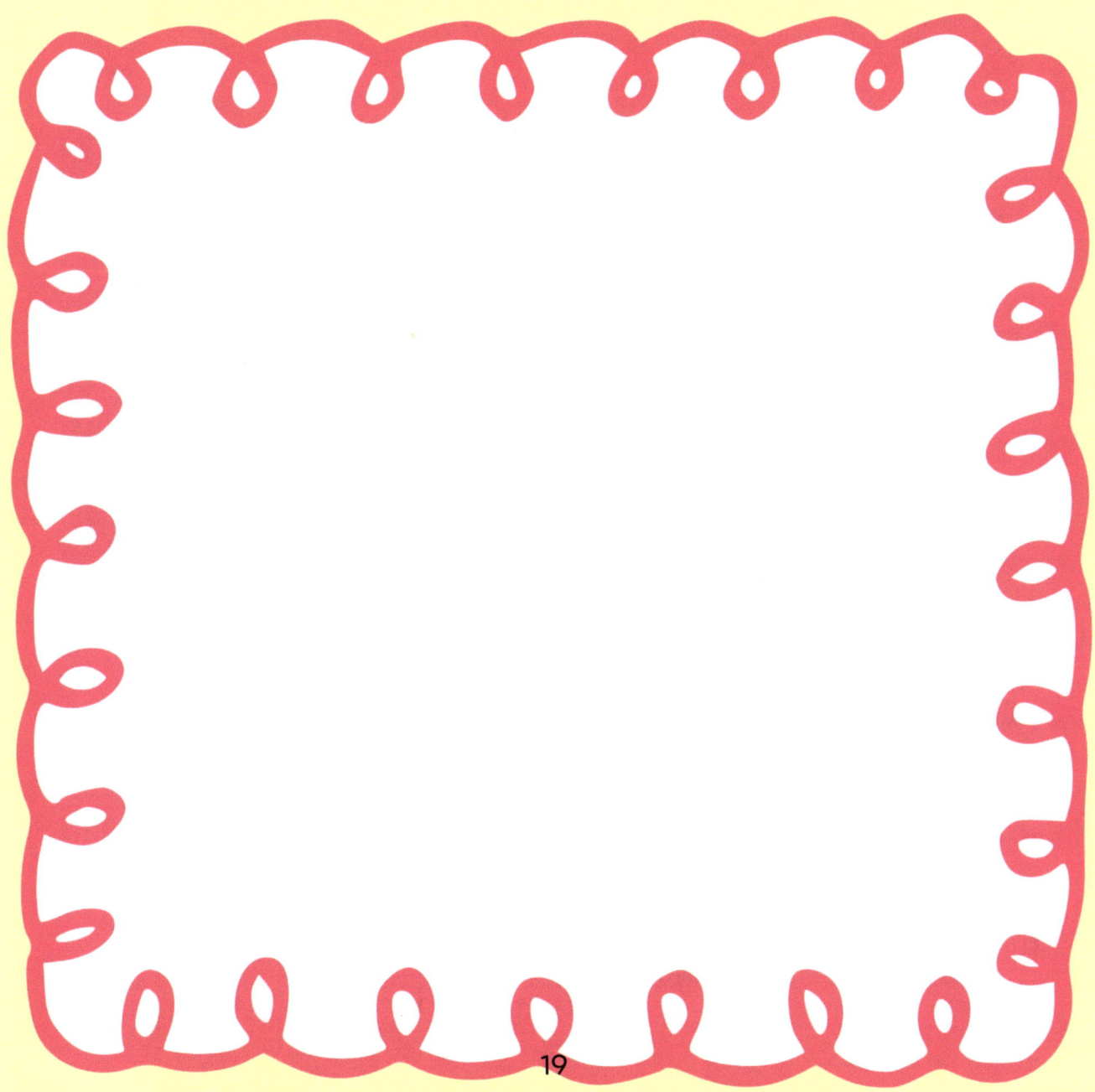

About Julie Fitzgerald

Julie Fitzgerald leads with love—for her family, her friends, and the moments they share together. Whether she's laughing until her sides hurt or simply being present, she cherishes connection above all.

Diagnosed with Young Onset Parkinson's disease, Julie has turned her personal experience into a mission of advocacy and empowerment. She's passionate about raising awareness, pushing for better care, and fighting for increased research funding. Julie volunteers with the Davis Phinney Foundation, the Michael J. Fox Foundation, the World Parkinson's Coalition, and Drive Towards a Cure. Her mission is simple: to "pay it forward" by offering strength, knowledge, and hope to others living with Parkinson's.

What drives Julie is connection, purpose, and doing things she once thought impossible. She loves to dance, sing, explore new places, and spend time with her dog, Hope, and cat, Peaches.

www.JulieForParkinsons.com

About Jayla Perez

Jayla is now ten years old and in fifth grade. She was recently accepted into the gifted program for the upcoming school year. Jayla is not only incredibly smart but also has a big heart. She's a very social kid with many friends, both at school and in her neighborhood.

She still loves building with Legos and playing the video game. Swimming is another favorite activity—she'll spend as much time as possible in the pool during the hot summer months.

Exciting news: Jayla and her parents traveled to the Philippines and have recently moved into their own home! They're all settling in wonderfully and are very happy.

About the Illustrator

Elena Stowell is an award-winning author, illustrator, and passionate Brazilian jiu-jitsu practitioner. When she isn't crafting stories, she's creating mixed-media illustrations, happily surrounded by paper scraps, dried paint, and glue sticks.

Elena is the author of *Flowing with the Go: A Jiu-Jitsu Journey of the Soul*, the children's books *Frango & Chicken* and *The Knotting Tree*, and co-founder of the Carly Stowell Foundation. Through her creative work and volunteer efforts, Elena strives to break down barriers, helping others overcome adversity and find hope through meaningful engagement in sports, music, and art.

www.elenastowell.com

www.ingramcontent.com/pod-product-compliance
Lightning Source LLC
Chambersburg PA
CBHW041447120626
46547CB00002B/373